THE
Plastic
MAGICIAN

THE
Plastic
MAGICIAN

RONNIE BERKE

XULON PRESS

Xulon Press
2301 Lucien Way #415
Maitland, FL 32751
407.339.4217
www.xulonpress.com

Printed in the United States of America.

Paperback ISBN-13: 978-1-6628-1188-3
Ebook ISBN-13: 978-1-6628-1189-0

In memory of my beautiful parents,
Edith and Al Berkowitz.

Special thanks to Guy Chaifetz for his help in editing,
researching the book and designing the front cover.

TABLE OF CONTENTS

INTRODUCTION

I'VE MET A lot of inmates and heard a lot of stories from some of the greatest criminal minds and con artists you can imagine in my seven years of incarceration in six different federal institutions. Arturo impressed me the first time I met him in Tallahassee Federal Prison in 1983. When asking him for the time, I couldn't help but notice his Patek Philippe special edition watch, costing thousands of dollars. Earlier I heard him speaking in three different languages with other inmates playing negotiator and interpreter. Together, we spent thirty days in solitary confinement for dirty urine samples which came back positive for marijuana. This enabled me to get to know him even better and to ultimately write his incredible life story up to his incarceration in 1983.

I had my doubts as to the validity of some of the schemes he pulled off, as I had heard so many before. After reading the front-page article from the Miami Herald about him ripping off American Express for $8,000,000.00, I was believing him a little bit more.

Bill would allow
optomerists to
prescribe drugs

LEGISLATIVE NEWS, PAGE 8A

Star Island life:
Pay for privacy,
and get publicity

LIVING TODAY, PAGE 1E

Tracy Austin
loses in Paris;
McEnroe wins

SPORTS NEWS, PAGE 1D

Cloudy,
Rain
Details on 2A

The Miami Herald

Home
Final
Edition

56 pages

Tuesday, May 31, 1983

25 cents

Credit-card fraud thrives in S. Florida

By JOE STARITA
Herald Staff Writer

In June 1982, shortly after they opened a makeshift office in Naples, Arthur Hoyos and Felix Suarez placed a small ad in The Wall Street Journal. It proved to be a boon for the two Miami men.

Before long, hundreds of total strangers from New York to California had helped Hoyos and Suarez buy $300,000 homes complete with swimming pools, plush furnishings, paintings and statues. The pair bought gold jewelry, a fancy Mercedes and a sporty Jaguar. They bought their secretary a new BMW. There were gambling junkets to Las Vegas

'This year, the projected loss in Dade County alone is expected to be between $6 million and $7 million It is a tremendous problem and one that is blossoming rapidly.'

Metro-Dade Sgt. Arthur Stack

and fat overseas bank accounts.

In one eight-day stretch alone, Metro-Dade police detectives estimate, the two men's elaborate

it was ever recovered," said Detective Alex Ortega, one of several investigators who helped convict the two men on numerous federal and state charges.

Last December, Hoyos, 34, and Suarez, 25, began serving eight- and six-year prison terms respectively.

Although caught and convicted, the two men and their rags-to-riches scheme underscores what has become a national nightmare for many banks, business people, credit-card companies and their

credit-card scam netted $250,000 in cash.

"They acquired a helluva nest egg in a very short time — possibly in the millions — and none of

Please turn to CREDIT / 4A

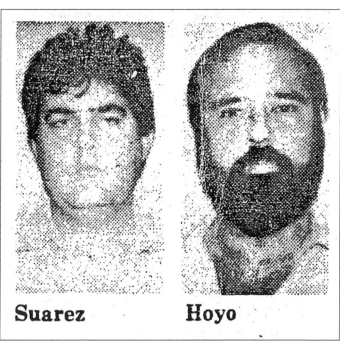

Suarez   Hoyo

One thing I know for sure, money and big balls can buy and change people. Arturo Hoyo had both. Coupled with the driving force of revenging his parents' death at the hands of a greedy businessman, he was destined to succeed. Being a true gentleman who speaks four different languages and a real class act doesn't hurt either. In fact, it made it easier to persuade and influence people that he was the real deal.

What I can't believe is how a person can change and assume a different identity as fast as it takes to take a bathroom break, or Clark Kent changing into Superman in a telephone booth. What kind of person is this and what kind of life is it to live? Being a different person and having a different identity for as long as it takes to run a scam? Does he ever go back to just being Arturo Hoyo? Can he accept that name, land a successful job and live a life of anonymity? Knowing him, I don't think so, for the sparkle in his eyes when he talks about playing and preparing for a new character in his exciting games of The Great Imposter and Who Do You Trust says, "No way."

Well, it all remains to be seen. Who, what and where will he end up next upon his release is anyone's guess? Although we did plan to get together upon his release in five years, a lot can happen in that period of time. Where will I be and if he gets in touch with me is anyone's guess as well. One thing is certain. He is the most interesting, unique and memorable person I have ever met. Still I wonder. Is he for real? Will I ever see him again?

Can It Be? No, It Can't. Is That Really You?

Chapter I

Revenging the Murder of His Parents

IN THE WORLD of credit cards and computers, the technical advances of rapid services are more sophisticated than ever, and without these services the banking world would never have advanced as far and as fast as it did. It was in this environmental setting that the banking community encountered their greatest nightmare. For he could wreck more havoc than Bonnie and Clyde and John Dillinger combined. But his tools of the trade didn't include submachine guns or Colt .45 automatics. No, his weapons were more of the sophisticated kind, that of the telephone and the ever-flexible, durable plastic credit card.

To them he was a wizard, The Plastic Magician. To the underworld, his name was spoken with envy and awe. He was able to dismantle banks and other companies and put them out of business with the ease that you or I go and buy gifts for other people's birthdays. Yes, he was the Phoenix, The Plastic Magician and the Wizard of Plastic Money. Born one Arturo Hoyo, a likeable man of Cuban descent, who arrived in this country in the early 60's. He showed the world what he could do and put his name on the front pages of every major newspaper, as one of the greatest con artists of the twentieth century to date. This is his story, so incredible, you may not think it's true.

Born into an upper-class family in Cuba, Arturo's father saw what the future held in store with the upcoming Castro Regime and sent his two sons to the safety of America. He put them in the hands of a trusted friend and business associate, one Enzo Del Bufalo. He feared that because of his political connections with Batista, Castro would go to any extreme to destroy and deteriorate him and his family's credibility and dignity in his homeland.

His perception and intuition couldn't have been more on the money. Five days later, after Senior Bufalo had accepted the boys and the millions that Arturo's father entrusted to him to set up a trust fund for the family. The family limousine that they were riding in was blown up, along with their estate. Arturo's whole family was murdered by the hands of their nemesis Fidel Castro, or so Arturo Hoyo thought at the time. It wasn't until seventeen years later that the true story of Arturo's family's murder was revealed to Arturo by the family's chauffeur, after an unexpected reunion in Miami between the two which led to physical persuasion or extortion tactics provided by Arturo Hoyo himself.

It seems that Senior Bufalo went to Havana and picked up Arturo and his brother, along with an undisclosed amount of money from Arturo's father. The father expressed his plans to Senior Bufalo, that he wanted his sons and the money out of Cuba in case he had difficulty with the new regime. At least his sons and some of his money would already be in the United States with a safe trust fund for the family. So Senior Bufalo checked himself and the two boys into the Fontainebleau Hotel in Miami Beach. Five days later there was no sign of Senior Bufalo or the money. That coupled with the death of the family a few days later, sent the two boys to separate foster homes. At the airport, Arturo turned to his brother crying out of control and said, "Someday we will get that man and out of all the ashes the Phoenix will be born again. I promise you we'll get him." The Phoenix being the name given to the family's sugar cane plantation in Cuba which was handed down from one generation to another.

By 1970, eleven years after his departure from Miami, Arturo found himself back in Miami as a salesman for a large tire corporation with exports to Central and South America. Little did he know, he was on the right road to finding the one person he so much hated. The only reason for his drive to be a success was the annihilation of one Enzo Del Bufalo.

It was 1972 and Arturo had grown with the company and prospered, to the point where he was their leading salesman and was traveling all over the world, but mostly to Central and South America. One day in late September, Arturo's company received a proforma from the largest importers of tires in Brazil, wanting to purchase a large government order of tires.

Arturo left for Brazil the following morning to secure the letter of credit which he, at the time, would never have believed would be the start of his illustrious career as a con artist and bring him closer to his long-awaited goal of finding the elusive Enzo Del Bufalo. When he arrived at the office of ZZ Enterprises in Brazil, he was confronted by the secretary who told him Mr. Antriotti was out for lunch and would be back in fifteen minutes. So, Arturo went to the lounge for some coffee and waited for Mr. Antriotti, the president of the largest import company of tires in Brazil.

When the intercom above Arturo sounded its request that Mr. Antriotti was ready to see him in his second-floor office, Arturo headed for the elevator with coffee still in his hand. When the elevator opened on the second floor, Arturo found himself face to face with Enzo Del Bufalo or was it? Arturo found himself in a state of shock and his adrenaline rose to the point of exploding, that the spilling of hot coffee all over his leg had no effect on him. Sure, it had been seventeen years, and time can play tricks on one's mind when fear and shock set in, but that was one face he would never forget no matter how many years and changes that person went through. How many dreams did he have where that face was as vivid as the picture of his parents that he kept in his wallet?

The silence was broken by a passerby who acknowledged Mr. Antriotti's presence by calling him Enzo. Now rage and loathing replaced the fear and shock, for now he knew for certain that the man in front of him, although the last name was different, was his long sought-after enemy, the ever-elusive Enzo Del Bufalo. There was no sign that Mr. Antriotti suspected who was seated in his office. For the boy he deserted seventeen years ago was a man now and was using a bogus name.

Realizing who the man he was dealing with and never letting his feelings show, it took all of Arturo's will power not to reach over the desk and choke the life out of the man who murdered his family and stole the family's fortune which was used for his escape to Brazil, and the founding of the largest import company in Brazil.

His time for revenge was now closer than ever. He wanted to do it right and make it work for himself. After the brief meeting, which didn't accomplish much, Arturo excused himself and made an appointment for the following morning blaming his fatigue on his long flight. Although his head was filled with thoughts of revenge that kept him going for seventeen years, he wasn't going to blow it now. He needed time to think and the answers would come sooner than he would have thought. Back at his hotel room, he called the airlines and made a reservation for the first flight out in the morning. He couldn't control his craving for revenge and his only thought was leaving Brazil as fast as possible with an excuse for breaking his appointment being a death in the family.

Back in the United States and on more familiar ground, Arturo's thoughts turned to his brother. Certainly, he too would be as elated as he was. The discovery of a long-awaited dream that was so close at hand. After reaching his brother at home and arranging a meeting at Arturo's apartment, Arturo proceeded to call the company and offer them an excuse for his abrupt departure from Brazil without securing the order.

Upon speaking to his boss, he was informed that he was fired from the job for leaving the country without contacting them first as to his reason why he left. It was an order his boss didn't want to blow and it would take at least a month to arrange another meeting in Brazil with Mr. Antriotti. Arturo's head was spinning from the prospect of losing his adversary. After coming so far and having been at arm's reach was alarming, the very thought that was unthinkable.

No one was going to stop his craving for revenge, for without that life had no meaning. On his way home to meet his brother, he stopped at a newsstand for a Miami Herald in hopes of securing another job. Unbeknownst to him at the time, that paper was going to unlock the door that had just closed on him and reveal all the answers he ever needed, in plotting his future endeavors, namely the con game.

After disclosing the sequence of events which took place in the undercovering of their adversary to his brother, Arturo sensed a feeling of accomplishment from Felix and from within himself. Although they still had a long way to go in achieving their goal in the demise of Enzo Del Bufalo, they were closer than ever before.

Within minutes of silent thought, brother Felix blurted out, "Why can't our company sell him tires?"

Arturo turned and said, "What company? I've been fired. There is no company." After an extended stare and a pose which seem like hours, Arturo said, "You're right, we'll start our own company and we'll call it The Commitment Tire Co."

This was the start of a con game that would blossom into an illustrious career of con schemes that would catapult one Arturo Hoyo to the front pages of the very newspaper that helped him achieve the goal of his life.

Being methodical and using calculated moves, the brothers put their plan into effect within one week, thanks to the aid of the classified section of the Miami Herald. First, by obtaining the lease of a warehouse, then a printer for their personalized stationery, a corporate lawyer to form the bogus corporation and then to the bank to deposit all the money they could muster up which amounted to ten thousand dollars, a petty sum considering they were going after millions.

Arturo was acting on the premise that the magnitude of the tremendous order of over $2,000,000.00 of all sizes of tires, which was a government order, could not be met by Arturo's ex-company. For the prices had to be right and Arturo knew better than most people just how shrewd a businessman Enzo Del Bufalo, alias Enzo Antriotti, was. Arturo would make him an offer he couldn't refuse for no one could beat his prices.

All the wheels were in motion and the "sting" was ready to be put into effect. After preparing a special price list which was 15% below wholesale, he sent it to ZZ Enterprises in Brazil attached with a note saying we can handle any size order. Two weeks later, a reply was received at the warehouse with a request for other prices for a special tire that wasn't contained in the original price list. After obtaining that information, Arturo felt a call to Brazil was in order, for the bait had been taken.

When he reached the office of ZZ Enterprises, the secretary had informed Arturo that Mr. Antriotti was leaving for the United States in the morning to check out a new company and their warehouse, for he was greatly interested in placing the government order with them, but only upon viewing your premises.

Hit with the situation that they never anticipated, they had to act fast and secure an inventory to impress their one and only client. Again, Arturo rose to the occasion by suggesting they engage the services of a national tire distributor that had an inventory second to none. Arturo was amazed at the confidence and spontaneity in which he was able to derive answers in a deadly scheme that he was a novice at. That was the answer and his life was on the line for if he failed and Enzo Del Bufalo found out his identity, he would share the same fate as that of his parents.

He set out to the tire company which he knew of from his experiences in that field for over six years. With plan in hand and a one out of ten chance in pulling it off, he approached the manager with three thousand dollars in his pocket and a story of a sheer genius. The story being he was an independent salesman who did a lot of business in South America and had brokered all of his own deals. "We have a very important customer coming from Brazil tomorrow and since the order is so large, I don't want to blow the deal. Unless he feels that I work for this company, he'll go somewhere else." Arturo stated that his warehouse didn't contain the inventory to impress his client. "I'll give you three thousand upfront to show you I'm dead serious, that a sale will take place, if I can just use your facility as that of one which I work for. (Let it be noted by this time Arturo had informed Mr. Antriotti of his change of companies when he was fired, reasons of a better position and more money. The new company being the Commitment Tire Company.)

"There is one more condition that has to be agreed on and this is the most important one," Arturo said, emotionally sensing he had the manager's approval already. "Let me paint the outside of the warehouse with the name of the company he thinks I work for, on the front. I promise I'll repaint it within the hour after he leaves at my own expense.

Luck and coincidence, along with fate, were on Arturo's side. For tomorrow would be Saturday, and the boss wouldn't be back to the warehouse until Monday. When Arturo took the three thousand dollars from his pocket and placed it on the manager's desk, Arturo knew he had pulled off the most incredible part of his impromptu scheme. The manager grabbed the money, shook his head and said, "For your sake, I hope it works and make sure this place is repainted by Sunday."

Within an hour, Arturo found himself at the painters' union rounding up a skeleton crew to do the job after flashing hundred-dollar bills in five painters' faces. He was able to secure both paint jobs for $2,800. Then it was back to the Commitment Tire Company to tell his brother the good news along with picking up their own stationery and letterheads coupled with some personal pictures of Arturo and his family of four. Everything was in place now, and only the arrival of the adversary was left.

The following morning, Arturo and his brother were at Miami International Airport waiting at the customs reception area for about five minutes when a familiar figure came through the electric doors. As the man stood there distracted, looking at the monitor that was projecting the arrival and departure times, Felix turned to Arturo and with a disbelieving look on his face said, "Don't you recognize that man?" After a long stare, Arturo still drew a blank. "You know who he is, it's Manuel, the goddamn chauffeur."

"That's impossible," Arturo said, for he was killed when our parents' limousine was blown up. But it was true, and Felix knew it the moment he laid eyes on him, and after observing him for about five minutes, Arturo too knew it was their parents' chauffeur of ten years. How could he forget as he knew him since birth? What was he doing here? "Maybe he can tell us how our parents died. Let's go and ask him," Arturo said.

Just as they were about to introduce themselves, Enzo walked out of the boarding gate with a surprised look on his face that startled Arturo. He thought Enzo recognized Felix but that was impossible for Felix had changed even more than Arturo had. Enzo approached the group and asked, "What are you doing here?" Arturo spoke out by saying, "Your secretary told me you were arriving today when I called your office on Friday to give you the prices you asked for."

Arturo was still puzzled as to the relationship between Manuel and Enzo Del Bufalo, but that answer was given by the introduction from Enzo. Manuel was going to be his forwarding agent and the person he would be dealing with in the states. Still, Arturo was puzzled as to the relationship between Manuel and Enzo and how it started, but now wasn't the time to wonder why. Now was the time for business, and everything was ready for the big sting. The long-awaited goal was about to come true and was only hours away. The taste of revenge was tasting sweet to Arturo and Felix.

When they arrived at their newly converted warehouse, Arturo could see that Enzo was quite impressed at the enormous structure which housed an inventory of over a million dollars-worth of tires. Going straight to their makeshift office of the manager who made all of this possible, Arturo felt right at home. For after six years as the leading salesman with his ex-company, this part of the scheme would be a breeze, and it was.

After a short tour of the facility, Enzo and Manuel were more than impressed with what they saw. Enzo now felt that $2,200,000.00 order could be easily handled by Arturo. Back in the office, Arturo drew up the paperwork on his bogus company letter head and it was signed only two hours after their arrival at the warehouse. Enzo Antriotti told Arturo that the letter of credit would be at their bank on Tuesday at the latest. After the shaking of hands which culminated the first part of the sting, it was now time to implement phase two of the operation.

After their departure, Arturo quickly contacted the painters and the manager to inform him of the sale he had made possible. Now they had to gather close to four hundred thousand pounds of used and wrecked machinery, or anything else that had good weight to substitute for the weight of tires. In other words, total garbage that was going to be placed in sealed containers for their ocean voyage to Brazil. This part of phase two wasn't going to be easy as Arturo thought, for it involved man power and vehicles of which he had neither.

With funds running low and good labor expensive, Arturo and Felix found themselves in little Havana bars gathering up whoever they could for $50.00 a day, which amounts to about twelve hours of back breaking work. Then he had to rent heavy equipment, which consisted of dump trucks, flat beds, fork-lifts and two semi-trailers, all requiring large deposits. Now they were ready to make the rounds to the various car wreck yards, car compressing plants and heavy machinery grave yards. They even found themselves at an airplane cemetery at the Opa Locka airport which yielded heavy scraps from dismantled planes.

After a week of solid work and only a thousand dollars left to their names, they had twenty-two containers filled with garbage. Now all that remained was the weigh-in on the ship dock and to be sealed by the forwarding agent which was Manuel. That was going to be the fun part and the revealing of the mystery behind their parents' death.

Arturo called Manuel at his office telling him everything was ready and all that was needed now was his signature and the viewing of the tires. He then gave him the address of their original warehouse which had held the bogus shipping containers.

Upon Manuel's arrival at the warehouse, he was ushered into an empty office which was void of any business equipment or furniture. Felix and Arturo surrounded Manuel with looks that could kill and a .380 Beretta in Arturo's hand. After revealing their true identities, Manuel, their parents' chauffeur of ten years, was faced with a life or death situation, and one which sent him to his knees. Begging for mercy he pleaded, "Spare me, Please! I had nothing to do with your parents' death and I couldn't stop it from happening for my life was at stake. It was Enzo who paid two of Castro's guerillas to place a bomb in the limousine. All I did was run from it when I opened the gate to the estate. Believe me, I loved your parents, but the money your father gave him made him go crazy. He made me work for him since then, so he could keep an eye on me. Let me live, I'll do anything you say, Please! Please! I don't want to die."

At that time, Arturo offered him a way out. "You sign all the papers, seal the containers, help us get the money out of the bank and then I want you to pull a Harry Houdini and disappear. We have three weeks to draw out $2,200,000.00. Hopefully, we'll get a good amount out before the ship arrives in Brazil and our scheme is found out."

With numerous trips to the bank, Arturo was able to withdraw all of the money before time ran out. Arturo and his brother couldn't believe they had pulled off the scam of their lives, along with the long-awaited revenge of Enzo Del Bufalo. Although this was just the start for Arturo, his brother, on the other hand, had enough of the con games and ended his career contented and financially comfortable. But for Arturo, the ease in which he was able to set this con game up was truly mind blowing. A good way to make big money and big money he made as you will see. But now, he had to get away for a while and enjoy the money he had made. Most of all, he didn't want any repercussions from Enzo, although he was sure that after Manuel told Enzo who they were, he would be happy to pay two million dollars in exchange for his life.

Chapter II

THE GRAND SCAMS OF THE PLASTIC MAGICIAN

SO IT WAS off to Madrid, Spain with his family, and for seven months he travelled throughout Europe, living like a king. It was in Europe where he realized the true value and importance of credit cards, of which he had none. For everywhere he checked into hotels and restaurants, the ever-changing currency was a hassle and could be avoided with "plastic money." When he returned to the United States seven months later with roughly $1,000,000.00, he started playing the role of a con man. The only difference being this role was for real.

By 1980, his fame had spread and people came to him from different states and other countries seeking advice on various frauds for a fee of $100,000.00. In 1981, Arturo owned a boiler room operation selling coal over the telephone. That business, which was operating in many states, sold a combined total of 25,000,000 non-existing futures, although Arturo's share was considerably less. Not a penny of that money has ever showed up, and the affair is still being investigated by the F.B.I. One agent is quoted as saying, "He's a pirate of the twentieth century who steals with his brain and a smile on his face, but when you meet him, you like him."

Sometimes, banks were part of his schemes in Florida: Barnett Bank, The Bank of Miami, Royal Trust Bank, Republic National Bank and many more. One bank official said that Arturo went to his bank in 1981 as an Argentinian Junta General and planned a very sophisticated fraud, involving the placement of $1,000,000.00 of his own money and representing the Argentinian government as one of their generals. This was a prearranged setup in which Arturo was able to secure official letterheads from the Argentinian Armed Forces. Then, he sent the official letter to the bank, announcing the arrival of one General Martinez, for procuring an account to be used for buying arms and supplies for their government, for their conflict between Argentina and Great Britain involving the Falkland Islands dispute.

Three days after he deposited the $1,000,000.00, he deposited a bogus cashier's check for over $6,000,000.00. When it was over the bank lost $2,500,000.00. He was able to do this because of information provided to him from big-time drug dealers from Cuba who were using the same bank for the laundering of drug money. Since the bank was being investigated for their involvement, they couldn't afford another scandal, so the bank took the loss of another successful sting operation.

In 1982, two more bank stings were done in Miami. Arturo opened an office on Kendall Drive and became a medical doctor, and promptly the banks lent him over $100,000.00 to purchase X-Ray equipment. That sting netted him $500,000.00 on a $10,000.00 investment within a month. Truly amazing it was, but he wasn't happy. So, he tried once more, and this one was the crème de la crème which put him on the front pages of every nationally known newspaper. It was this sting operation which gave him the name, "The Plastic Magician."

Arturo doesn't spend all his time running con games and sting operations. He does manage time in between scams to travel all over the world, sometimes even with the Jet-Set. He is always seen wearing his Gucci shoes and his Patek Phillippe watch. His manner always as a "Spanish Senior" with a $500,000.00 home in Miami, an apartment in Hawaii and a winter home in Monaco. He drives a Jaguar and a Mercedes. His beautiful wife and two children can be seen with him on most occasions. There were times when he was seen with Goldie Hawn in the Bahamas, thought to be a romance. He is suave and cool with millions to turn everyone inside out. With his impromptu trips to New York, London and Paris, in nothing less than a Learjet, which is always at his disposal.

In the beginning of 1982, while changing schemes every time a new sting started to unfold, Arturo began a scheme which he had been planning ever since his trip to Europe in 1977. Now he was ready, and after dealing with the banks and being successful, he had all the confidence in the world. His target was American Express. To them, Arturo Hoyo became their greatest nightmare. For at one time, in one of his many make shift offices that he had throughout South Florida, Arturo was making an average of $250,000.00 dollars a week. American Express does not want to talk about how much they lost, they pretend not to know. There are some individuals within American Express who estimate that they lost between five and ten million in an eight-month period. Now that's a sting. That's why I saved the best one for last.

Arturo started by purchasing an existing car rental company for $250,000.00, which had twenty-five cars in the parking lot. Then he proceeded to open an electronics company called American National Electronics which was a mail order company with offices in Naples and Miami. Next, Arturo sold off the twenty-five cars for $175,000.00, for he never planned on renting them out. He was only using their validating machine for credit cards and the company's good credit standing with American Express for the past six years. Then he placed an ad in the Wall Street Journal, selling cut rate deals on Sony televisions, Sony Walkmans and Atari video games.

Within two weeks, more than six hundred customers placed their orders providing Arturo with real names, addresses and credit card numbers. Then he bought sheets of plain white plastic and an embossing machine. He started using the rent-a-car business near Miami International Airport where it all started five years before, when Enzo Del Bufalo and Manuel helped put him in this financial position. With the names and numbers gathered from the Wall Street Journal ad, Arturo used the plastic to fashion phony credit cards, embossed with legitimate names and numbers. Then he sent American Express hundreds of invoices for rental car bills. American Express paid Arturo, then billed unwitting cardholders across the country, many of whom had never been to Florida.

By the time American Express got word of what had happened, boom, the whole thing was a bust, and Arturo was gone. Meanwhile the losses for American Express piled up, and with the exception of New York, nowhere were credit card losses piling up as fast as in Florida. In one eight day stretch alone, the scam netted $250,000.00.

One of the ways for Arturo to get all the money out of the banks was to buy Krugerrands. Of the $25,000,000 lost nationwide by American Express that year, about $4,200,000 was racked up in Florida. Your guess is as good as mine as to how much Arturo Hoyo was responsible for. Knowing him like I do, and believe me, I know him, for he confided in me to the point I had to write his incredible story, so I'd say he accounted for $3,000,000. There was one individual who he charged $90,000.00 for a rent-a-car, and that person never was in Florida.

The end of Arturo Hoyo's con games and sting operations came to a close in October of 1982 when a business associate, John Egner, was arrested in a Miami bank, taking money out of one of Arturo's con accounts. Later, attorney Stuart Mishkin and John Egner blackmailed Arturo for $50,000.00. After he paid them, they still turned Federal and State witness and they received immunity for turning on the Phoenix.

After his arrest, he plead guilty in a plea bargain to one State count and two Federal counts and the other fifty-two counts were dropped. He was sentenced to eight years in a Federal prison on all fraud related charges. After his conviction, one thing should be clear to the American people. Credit card companies and the banking institutions even with their millions of sophisticated computers couldn't stop one man, Arturo Hoyo, alias "The Plastic Magician." Why didn't anyone have the answers that Arturo had?

When Miami detective Alex Ortega, who arrested Arturo and who also testified as well said of the con man, "When they made the mold of a con man, they used Arturo Hoyo."

When asked what he did with all the millions, Arturo simply said, "I spent it all," with a straight face. Although detective Ortega doesn't believe that to be true, he stated, "Oh, he has a whole pile of money stashed somewhere. We know exactly where it is. We're just unable to go and retrieve it."

How is it that, even in a Federal prison in Tallahassee, Florida, where he can only spend $90.00 a month for his commissary and a paycheck of $4.40 a week or $0.11 an hour, where his life has changed drastically, his looks and demeanor haven't changed much under the circumstances. After ten minutes into a conversation, you can't help but like him and envy his warehouse of knowledge. He's your twentieth century con artist hero, with adventures and romances, coupled with his millions, that only we peasants can dream of doing. EF Hutton has nothing over The Plastic Magician, for when he speaks, everyone listens, because everything he says sounds like it's coming from the best-selling book about How To Make Money Without Really Trying, and we all want to know the answer to that question. But we won't get any more answers from Arturo for a while, for he should be at peace with himself, and the outside world too now that he's in prison, you would think.

No, even in prison he couldn't find sanctuary from the outside world, for because of his expertise in the ever-changing world of credit cards and credit lines, his style and knowledge was the most sought after by the establishments higher echelon, namely the major banking institutions and the major credit card companies.

On several occasions, he received letters from Vice President George Bush and Congressmen Dante Fascell, who were able to appeal to his strong ego and his insuppressible amount of confidence. He soon found his way in front of the Judiciary Subcommittee on Crime in Washington, D.C. involving con schemes. He was quoted as saying, "Plastic money is a real cancer that is growing daily and posing ever greater attraction for criminals."

He wasn't telling them anything they didn't know already and because of that appearance, his popularity grew more with the credit card companies and banks and less with the criminal underworld. Although he was given immunity, no names were given, only his methods were revealed. Since that hearing, Arturo Hoyo has received numerous proposals from various lending institutions and credit card companies wanting to hire him as a consultant and trouble shooter for their companies. But Arturo Hoyo won't make a decision yet, for he still has two years left on his 8-year sentence.

One thing is for certain, the "Phoenix," "The Plastic Magician", will fly again, Whether or not the Federal Government did its job and rehabilitated him is anyone's guess. Until that time when he gets set free to fly and proceed with his future plans, the banking world and the credit card companies will hold their breath and pray that when he lands, it will be on the side of justice and law and order. For if not, they're in for another earth-shattering experience and one they can ill afford. Only Arturo Hoyo, alias the "Plastic Magician," knows for sure what the future holds in store.

Can It Be? No, It Can't. Is That Really You?

In November of 1988, I found myself working for two of the biggest gentlemen's clubs in South Florida called The Dollhouse and Solid Gold. I started working for them upon my release from prison in October 1986, thanks to a close friend who knew the owner Michael J. Peter. I worked as the day shift manager of Solid Gold in Fort Lauderdale. I couldn't work the night shift because I was on an electronic monitoring bracelet and had to be home by 9 p.m. for six months. This was a condition of my three years, special parole. Thank God I had six years taken off my sentence by doing my own appeal. Still, even the smallest of violations could land me back in prison for three years.

After six months, I was promoted to the night shift manager position of Dollhouse III in Pompano Beach, Florida, the biggest gentlemen's club in South Florida. It was where Motley Crue's hit song "Girls, Girls, Girls" in The Dollhouse in Fort Lauderdale derived from. I was there when they performed it live on stage at Dollhouse III. It looked like a huge flying saucer from the outside. I was in my glory, going to work every day, from celibacy of seven and a half years in federal prison to running the biggest gentlemen's club in south Florida, a dream come true.

I came out of prison to no family with three years left on my sentence of twenty-three years. I was starting over at forty-one years of age with no money, no family and only a house I was able to save which I bought under the Veterans Administration in 1973 for my parents' retirement and a couple close friends' help. Now I'm going forward with my new life, with a new attitude and outlook of making money the legal way. This job was a great beginning.

One Saturday night in November of 1988, I received a phone call from the owner of The Dollhouse telling me that Mr. Bacardi of the Bacardi Rum family was on his way to the club in the owner's private limo. My instructions were to comp his bill, put some of our best champagne on ice and put it in a private area of the VIP room. I informed my staff of his coming and for them to get everything ready and notify me upon his arrival. About twenty minutes later, I was notified that Mr. Bacardi's limo had just pulled up. By the time I got to the front entrance way, there were six or seven of our most beautiful women walking to the front door.

Surrounded by our loveliest ladies, the male figure coming through the door looked strikingly familiar to a person from my past. Can it be? No, it can't. Is that really you? The Plastic Magician, the one and only Arturo Hoyo has landed back into my life upon his release from prison as Mr. Bacardi? Wow! Unbelievable! My arms were full of goosebumps from instant recognition when Arturo's eyes met mine. There was no handshake. Our reaction being one of the same, found us in a bear hug that was sincere and long lasting. I whispered, "I can't believe it's you!

His reply, "I can't believe I found you! Don't say anything, I'll explain."

The look on my staff's faces was one of shock and bewilderment as I lead him to the VIP Room, still not believing what I was experiencing. One thing was for sure, my doubts of his past real-life impersonations was just put to rest, five years after writing his life story in a jail cell we shared for thirty days for positive urine samples for marijuana in F.C.I. Tallahassee in 1983. I couldn't wait to hear this story while walking to the VIP Room. Once in, he told me that he had the owner of The Dollhouse and Solid Gold believing that he's Mr.

Bacardi, and the owner was going to partner up with him and open a gentlemen's club in Germany. The owner was putting up more than half of the money, a little more than one million dollars. Then he said, "I'll disappear or now that I found you, I just might keep it a little while and have you run it for me."

I couldn't believe what I was hearing. But now wasn't the time to discuss my future as The Plastic Magician's sidekick and running partner. No, now was the time for celebration, and what better place than the biggest gentlemen's club in South Florida with some of the most beautiful women in the world dancing nude in a private booth with free champagne, the best that money can buy. Yes, this was the start of a night I would treasure and cherish forever.

After about two hours of champagne and his giving out over three thousand dollars in twenties to our beautiful staff who were entertaining him, we had very little time to talk in the VIP Room. I still had a club to run. His disguise and maintaining his character role as Mr. Bacardi were paramount, and he wasn't going to allow this chance meeting, or so I thought, between two old cellmates, to jeopardize his laid-out plan to rip off the owner of The Dollhouse for over a million dollars. At about 3 a.m., Arturo (Mr. Bacardi) told me he was leaving and wanted me to go with him. "We close at 5 a.m.," I told him, "and I'm the closing manager."

So, I will call you when I get off work." He said, "Call the owner and tell him I want you to take me to the new Solid Gold in Miami on 163rd Street and Biscayne Boulevard." I couldn't believe his request, but I had to call the owner, who I figured would say no, as only the assistant manager would be left to lock up on the busiest night of the week.

The owner's reply was shocking. He told me, "No problem. Give your keys to the assistant manager and have him lock up. if there is a problem, have him call you." I was also told to make sure the bill at Solid Gold is comped and show him a good time as he's going to be a future partner.

Well, I had just gotten the green light to celebrate with my friend Arturo, alias Mr. Bacardi, at the owner's expense. Three of our staff were persuaded to join our party who were getting off of work, thanks to a generous donation by Arturo who was also accompanied by two beautiful models. The trip to Solid Gold for the seven of us, which took about an hour, was a party in itself, with free champagne, good music and naked dancers entertaining Mr. Bacardi and me, I might add.

This was an incredible time and situation in my life and really had me thinking about my future as Arturo's sidekick and running partner. My head was in cloud nine and enjoying the moment, but I knew I would have to make a decision soon.

Going into Solid Gold was like going into another world, with the exotic and plush décor and motif, along with the service fit for a king. Arturo and the five women along with myself felt like royalty, with a homey feeling. The club was running drink specials all night with any Bacardi liquor with announcements coming from the DJ booth every half hour. The hour we had before the club closed was out of this world.

What a character Arturo picked to impersonate after five years in prison. So similar to where I wound up after seven and a half years. Arturo invited some of the women back to his hotel suite at the Fountainebleu Hotel in Miami Beach. I too was invited for the after party, that after party you're lucky if you can still walk, if you know what I mean, that ended well after the sun came up. This had been one incredible night and now day.

With my car being at The Dollhouse over an hour away, I wasn't able to leave until 3 p.m., as the limo was dropping off some of the women guests. Arturo, alias Mr. Bacardi, was playing his role to the max, with class and professionalism. All of which were part of his own personal characteristics that I admired, respected, and wrote about from the first day I met him five years ago. He was a true gentleman in real life and what he portrayed in Mr. Bacardi.

It was in the limo ride back to The Dollhouse to get my car with Arturo that I heard about the revelations that brought about our chance meeting at The Dollhouse, which was more than a chance meeting, but one of a calculated outcome. Arturo told me that word had gotten back to the prison and him in FCI Tallahassee where I did most of my time, a total of fifty-four months, as to where I was. He said when he heard that I was working for Solid Gold, he was happy for me and a bit jealous all at once. So, he decided he wanted to have a club like that of his own. That's how his plan was conceived, wanting to reunite with me and having his own gentlemen's club.

First, he had to locate me and convince me to go with him and run scams, starting with the owner of the biggest gentlemen's clubs in Florida. This was his plan upon release. He had past friendships with people throughout Europe and South America from his jet-setting years when making $250,000.00 a week thanks to Plastic Money. Money that was taken from unsuspected customers who gave their credit card numbers hoping to purchase Sony Trinitron TVs from a commercial Arturo ran selling them at cost at $200.00 each. Just to gather credit card numbers.

His friends in Germany helped him secure a building and someone knew a family member of the Bacardi Empire. So, he adopted the identity of Mr. Bacardi, knowing things about the family, which is par for the course, for whenever Arturo undertakes a role, a thorough investigation goes into effect, just like an actor preparing for a role in a movie. He knew he would locate me, as he knew I had special parole, so unless I got fired, he would locate me. He had to set the plan and impersonation in motion, even if he didn't locate me and convince me to go to Germany with him. Everything in Arturo's plan was predicated on ripping off the owner of The Dollhouse for as much money as he could, and over a million dollars was a nice amount of money for his start back into the world of the Great Imposter in the game of Who Do You Trust.

No, Arturo didn't learn his lesson. After five years, his old lifestyle won out. It's an addiction. I saw it in his eyes when I was writing his story. When he was explaining to me how he prepares and sets up his scams. I knew he couldn't go back to anonymity and live under his birthright name of Arthur Hoyo ever again. Wow, I couldn't believe what he just told me. This was a premeditated plan that would satisfy Arturo. One, he could reunite with me and continue the friendship we started. Second, it's a popular business that generates a lot of money, plus it has good fringe benefits. Now, I really have a decision to make and a quick one because Arturo was going back to Germany in days. That was all the time I had to make one of the biggest decisions of my life.

For the next three days, we saw or spoke to each other every day. Going out to dinner in some of the most expensive restaurants in Miami and Ft. Lauderdale, coupled with the night club scene, which Arturo took control of and wouldn't let me spend a dime. He was doing his best to convince me to go back to Germany with him and start a new life of the rich and famous, making money running scams all around the world. This was a life Arturo was very familiar with and he had proven he could excel in that world. Still, after five years in prison and coming out to millions that he stashed away, he didn't learn his lesson. The question for me was a simple one. What's my price for freedom? How much money would I need to have in the bank to give up my freedom again?

It took the Feds and the State of New York nine and a half years to put me away, which included three trials in that period of time. I too lived a life of the rich and famous, flying private jets and owning boats and planes while smuggling and selling cocaine to some of the top athletes and entertainers in Hollywood and in the music industry. I had Joe Namath's penthouse apartment with a pool right above me on the roof, for five years. I've had my fair share of excitement and beautiful women in my life. But after what the Feds put me through for ten and a half years, which is a story in itself, you could say prison didn't agree with me.

I made the best out of a bad situation, still doing things my way any time given the chance. It was just too many years of being unproductive in not making money for my future. But most importantly, the lack of sexual compatibility and relationships with the opposite sex that was the deciding factor. It was time for me to settle down and find a good woman and try to live without fear that I might get arrested for something I did to make money. Even if I would go with Arturo and would have to come back to the USA for any reason, whether I did anything wrong or not, they would see a warrant for my arrest for parole violation and escape, for a total of at least six more years in prison. No more making money illegally for me. No. I couldn't go with my friend Arturo and I gave up the chance to make millions and add more years of excitement to my life and hob-nob with the rich and famous again.

No, not with the fear of prison in the equation. Did that. Done that. I had to reach deep down in my heart and soul as to what I wanted out of life and what would truly make me happy. I knew Arturo would be disappointed and I probably wouldn't see him again, because he won't keep the club if I'm not with him. He will disappear into thin air like Harry Houdini and take on another character. I had my chance, but the timing wasn't right. If I was younger and didn't give the Government a total of fifteen and a half years of my life, including two years in Vietnam, I might have made a different decision.

Arturo was very disappointed when I gave him my decision, but I think he understood. We had a great time together in those three days. I was going to miss my close friend, who went through all those changes just to be with me and show me he was for real and wanted to share his life of the rich and famous with me. We had a final drink and a big, long bear hug at his hotel, wishing each other the best, and saying I'll see you again, stay in touch. But I was right. I never heard from Arturo again, nor did the owner of The Dollhouse ever contact me about Mr. Bacardi. What a great ending to an amazing story about the most memorable and interesting person I have ever met.

By Ronnie Berke

Chapter III

Testimony at the Senate Subcommittee On Crime, Washington D.C.

COUNTERFEIT ACCESS DEVICE AND COMPUTER FRAUD AND ABUSE ACT THURSDAY, SEPTEMBER 29, 1983 HOUSE OF REPRESENTATIVES, SUBCOMMITTEE ON CRIME, COMMITTEE ON THE JUDICIARY, Washington, DC.

THE SUBCOMMITTEE MET, pursuant to call, at 10:10 a.m., in room 2237, Rayburn House Office Building, Hon. William J. Hughes (chairman of the subcommittee) presiding.

Present: Representatives Hughes, Feighan, Smith, Shaw, and Sensenbrenner. Representative Fish Staff present: Hayden W. Gregory, counsel; Edward O'Connell, assistant counsel; Charlene Vanlier, associate counsel, and Phyllis N. Henderson, clerical staff.

Mr. HUGHES. The Subcommittee on Crime will come to order. The Chair has received a request to cover this hearing in whole or part by television broadcast, radio broadcast, still photography or by other similar methods. In accordance with committee rule 5(a), permission will be granted unless there is objection. Hearing no objection, coverage will be permitted.

Today we will receive testimony on the problems relating to credit card fraud and counterfeiting and the related issue of computer-assisted crimes. I am sure it is not surprising to most of us that currency and even checks are becoming a diminishing part of our everyday life. Instead, we are increasingly becoming dependent on credit cards, computers, and other such devices. These technological advances have left our laws almost totally inadequate. In fact, we have good reason to believe that merely bringing our laws up to date by revising them to reflect present technology will not be adequate; for rapidly changing technology will leave them obsolete in another 5 or 10 years. Experts tell us that we need to shift attention in our statutes from concepts such as tangible property and possession to concepts of information and access to information. H.R. 3570, which Mr. Sawyer and I introduced on July 14th of this year, makes counterfeiting, producing, or possessing counterfeit-making equipment and credit cards if these illegal acts in the aggregate produce anything of value worth $5,000—within one year— or the defendant is in possession of ten or more counterfeit instruments indicating he or she is more than a small-time thief. It also expands a scope of this legislation to other computer-assisted crimes if they aggregate $5,000 in illegal gains in one year.

ADDITIONAL MATERIAL [From the Miami Herald, May 31, 1983] CREDIT-CARD FRAUD THRIVES IN SOUTH FLORIDA (By Joe Starita)

In June 1982, shortly after they opened a makeshift office in Naples, Arthur Hoyo and Felix Suarez placed a small ad in The Wall Street Journal. It proved to be quite a boon for the two Miamians. Before long, hundreds of total strangers from New York to California had helped Hoyo and Suarez buy $500,000 homes complete with swimming pools, plush furnishings, paintings and statues. The pair bought gold jewelry, a fancy Mercedes and a sporty Jaguar. They bought their secretary a new BMW. There were gambling junkets to Las Vegas and fat overseas bank accounts. In one eight-day stretch alone, Metro-Dade police detectives estimate, the two men's elaborate credit-card scam netted $250,000 in cash. "They acquired a helluva nest egg in a very short time—possibly in the millions— and none of it was ever recovered," said Detective Alex Ortega, one of several investigators who helped convict the two men on numerous federal and state charges. Last December, Hoyo, 34, and Suarez, 35, began serving eight- and six-year prison terms respectively. Although caught and convicted, the two men and their rags-to-riches scheme underscores what has become a national nightmare for many banks, business people, credit-card companies and their customers.

In 1982, according to a Congressional subcommittee that opened hearings on the issue last week, nationwide losses from credit-card fraud totaled a staggering $1 billion. "This year, the projected loss in Dade County alone is expected to be between $6 million and $7 million," said Metro-Dade Sgt. Arthur Stack, who heads the department's four-member credit-card squad. "It is a tremendous problem and one that is blossoming rapidly. I don't see an end in sight at this time." Police and prosecutors are quick to list a number of factors contributing to the phenomenal growth of America's illicit plastic empire. Without costly and extensive undercover investigations, credit-card swindlers often are difficult to detect and difficult to prosecute. Penalties frequently are lax. In South Florida, victimless crimes seldom warrant top priority.

Another key factor, authorities say, is the unwieldy credit-card bureaucracy itself. It allows slick white-collar criminals, like Hoyo and Suarez, to keep their operations one step ahead of the traditional 30- to 60-day billing cycles.

THE NEWSPAPER SCAM

In the Hoyo-Suarez scam, for example, the two men offered readers of The Wall Street Journal cut-rate deals on Sony Walkmans and Atari video games. Within two weeks, more than 600 customers placed their orders . . . credit-card numbers. The two men took the information, bought sheets of plain white plastic and an embossing machine and opened a Rent-a-Car business near Miami International Airport. Using the names and numbers gathered from The Wall Street Journal ad, Hoyo and Suarez used the plastic to fashion phony credit cards embossed with legitimate names and numbers. The two men then sent American Express hundreds of invoices for rental-car bills. American Express paid the two men, then billed unwitting card holders across the country, many of whom had never been to Florida. (191) 192 "By the time American Express got word of what had happened—boom—the thing was a bust and they [Hoyo and Suarez] were gone," said Detective Ortega. Meanwhile, the losses for American Express piled up. And with the exception of New York, nowhere are credit-card losses piling up faster than in Florida—particularly in Dade, Broward and Palm Beach counties.

FLORIDA NO. 2

Officials representing the major credit-card companies report that Florida ranks No. 2 in the nation—ahead of California and behind New York—in volume of dollars lost to fraudulent transactions. For example, of the $40 million lost in counterfeit transactions by Visa and MasterCard nationwide in 1982, $8 million—or 20 percent—occurred in Florida, said Arnold Wenzloff, vice president for security and recovery at Southeast Bank. Of the $25 million lost nationwide by American Express last year, about $4.2 million—or 17 percent—was racked up in Florida, a company spokesman said. "Probably a good 80 percent of the statewide losses are in South Florida,' Michael Quackenbush, president of Southeast Bank's Southeast Services. Credit-card fraud in Broward County is responsible for losses of at least $2 million a year to local businesses, police and prosecutors estimate.

Last year, only 64 persons were arrested in Broward for using stolen or counterfeit credit cards. Although that was nearly double the 35 arrested in 1981, police concede that the arrests represent only the tip of the iceberg. "Theoretically, there should have been at least 250 arrests last year and maybe a lot more than that," said Lt. Joseph Desantis, director of the Broward Sheriff's fraud-investigations unit. "They're just very tough to get, and when you get them, nothing happens to them," he said.

Mr. HUGHES. Our next witnesses are a panel that includes Detective Alex Ortega, who is with the Economic Crime Unit of Metro Dade Police Department in Miami, FL, and Mr. Arturo Hoyo, an incarcerated credit card violator at the Federal Correction Institute in Tallahassee. Detective Ortega has been with the Metro-Dade Police Department for some 3 years, the last year and a half of which has been with a special credit card section which was set up at the request of numerous Miami banks. Mr. Ortega owned his own business prior to his current police employment, and before that he was a security manager for a department store. Mr. Ortega obviously is well qualified to discuss credit card fraud. Mr. Hoyo is presently serving a sentence, as I have indicated, at a Federal correctional institute.

At this point I would like to make a few things clear. First, Mr. Hoyo is testifying before the Subcommittee on Crime purely on a voluntary basis and, as a matter of fact, at his own request. We asked the Federal Bureau of Prisons to make him available and they graciously acceded to our request in order to acquaint the committee with Mr. Hoyo's special knowledge of credit card fraud. We on the subcommittee have no intention of glorifying Mr. Hoyo for his criminal activity and, in fact, his present incarceration, I think it speaks loud and clear as to where criminal activity eventually leads: to institutionalization. Mr. Hoyo has indicated to the subcommittee a desire to partially redeem himself and stated in his own words that he has a profound knowledge of the various schemes used today to exploit credit card and other facets of the economy.

So, we welcome you as a panel. First, let's begin with you, Mr. Ortega. We have your statement and, without objection, will be made a part of the record. You may proceed as you see fit.

TESTIMONY OF ALEX ORTEGA, DETECTIVE, ECONOMIC CRIME UNIT, METRO-DADE POLICE DEPARTMENT, MIAMI, FL, AND ARTURO HOYO, NO. 10849–004, INCARCERATED CREDIT CARD VIOLATOR, FEDERAL CORRECTION INSTITUTE, TALLAHASSEE, FL

Mr. ORTEGA. I am here today basically to explain to the panel that the problems involved in credit card counterfeiting are increasingly growing throughout the United States, but more particularly in south Florida or in the State of Florida. If I may say, the cards you see before you there were made by a silk screen process. They were all imprinted with the Farrington embossing machine which I have brought one with me today. If you would like to see one, I will show it. The Metro-Dade Police Department, which put together a squad of detectives to specifically investigate credit card fraud, began over a year or so ago and since then we have noticed that cases seem to be coming in faster than we can handle them. It is a type of crime that is sophisticated and involves a growing number of people that came on the Mariel boatlift in 1980. It would be safe to say that 70 percent of the individuals involved in credit card fraud in the south Florida area were recent arrivals from the boatlift.

Now, we have noticed that, as in Mr. Hoyo's case, which was a special case that what he did, as we said earlier, would solicit advertisements in the Wall Street Journal. Mr. Hoyo, after he accumulated X number of account numbers, would then print them up on plain pieces of plastics, as you have before you there, with the machine. The large amount of the frauds that we have occurring now in south Florida is—

Mr. HUGHES. Are these the cards we have?

Mr. ORTEGA. Yes, sir.

Mr. HUGHES. You say you do have a machine with you?

Mr. ORTEGA. Yes, I do.

Mr. HUGHES. Can you show us what you are talking about so that we can view that as you are testifying?

Mr. ORTEGA. Sure.

Mr. HUGHES. Now, what does this machine actually do?

Mr. ORTEGA. This machine, what it actually does, it imprints the account numbers, names, and information that is on a legitimate credit card. It printed that one there.

Mr. HUGHES. It prints something like this?

Mr. ORTEGA. Yes, sir.

Mr. HUGHES. With the number and name?

Mr. ORTEGA. The name and the lettering and the numbers on there are very similar to the font style that is used by the industry, with the exception of a few numbers. If I may say, just 2 or 3 months ago, as our unit was making several arrests on manufacturers of these credit cards, the criminals involved in this type of organized crime broke into a business machine company where they sell these to any legitimate business. They broke in and they burglarized it and took six machines. Along with the embossing machines that were taken there was an encoder taken.

Now, an encoder is something where you can run the credit card through the mag strip that contains the account information on the cardholder; you can erase that information and put in new information, and you can continuously use the card over and over again. Now, that particular machine has not been recovered even though a few of the embossing machines have been recovered.

A major problem in south Florida and throughout the country, speaking to other police agencies, have been with an operation which is termed a "bust-out" operation. A "bust-out" operation is where a merchant just opens a business for the sole purpose of submitting fraudulent charges. They start a corporation under alias names; they open a bank account; and they submit an average of $80,000– $90,000 in a few weeks period before they close shop and disappear. The problem with the bust-out operations is that before the banks or the card-issuing banks realize that they are counterfeit, naturally the merchant has gone.

Mr. HUGHES. Mr. Hoyo, we welcome you also. I wonder if you would in general, without naming particular victims or credit card companies, tell us about your own activity in credit card fraud and possibly discuss the schemes that you are aware of, for example, how easy it is to institute these schemes.

Mr. HOYO. Mr. Chairman, I have one page here that I would like to read to you and then I would like to go ahead with the questions you have.

Mr. HUGHES. All right, sure.

Mr. HOYO. Mr. Chairman, distinguished members of the House subcommittee: A few words to introduce myself, and give you a brief outline of my past and the motive of my presence before you. My name is Arturo Hoyo. I am 35 years old, a Cuban by birth, and a naturalized citizen of this great country. Presently I am serving an 8-year sentence at the Federal Correctional Institution in Tallahassee, FL, and as a very important and vital part of my rehabilitation I appear before you.

In the past, and for the past 6 years, I have been involved in many different sophisticated frauds; some of them with credit cards. By 1980, I was considered by the criminal world one of the top sting artists in the United States. A variety of people came to me from other States and other countries to see me. They would approach me with their ideas and these ideas, if I felt they had any merit or could be improved, I would work out a deal at a minimum fee of $100,000, up front; then I would put it to practical use and improve on it if it was necessary.

Now, after realizing the wrongful past, I am changing my creativity to the right way. I would like to fight legally, using my talents, to get the white-collar criminals who are presently defrauding credit card companies and their innocent customers. Plastic money has become a national nightmare for many banks, business people, credit card companies, and their customers. Plastic money is a real cancer which is growing daily in the United States. It is more difficult to go to a bank in Miami and change a $100 check than do a "sting" on a credit card company and make a quarter of a million dollars in 8 days.

My only wish and desire is that in the near future I will not be known as the best sting artist that everyone said I was, but as the best specialist in fighting credit card frauds and other related frauds that I will be; so my family and my children can once be proud again of me. I am sure you are well aware of my notorious past; and with no reservation, I will try to help and answer all your questions. Thank you, Mr. Chairman.

[The statement of Mr. Hoyo follows:]

STATEMENT OF ARTURO HOYO

Mr. Chairman, distinguished members of the House subcommittee, a few words to introduce myself, and give you a brief outline of my past and the motive of my presence before you. My name is Arturo Hoyo, I am 35 years old, a Cuban by birth, and a naturalized citizen of this great country. Presently I am serving an 8-year sentence at the Federal Correctional Institution in Tallahassee, Florida, and as a very important and vital part of my rehabilitation I appear before you. In the past, and for 6 years, I have been involved in many different "sophisticated frauds"; some of them with credit cards. By 1980 I was considered by the criminal world one of the "top sting artists" in the United States.

A variety of people came to Miami from other States and countries to see me. They all approached me with their "ideas" and if I felt that these "ideas" had any merit or could be improved, I worked out a deal at a minimum fee of $100,000 up front; then I would put it to practical use and improve if it was necessary.

Now after realizing the wrongful past, I am changing my creativity to the right way. I would like to fight legally, using my talents, to get the white-collar criminals who are presently defrauding credit card companies and their innocent customers. "Plastic money" has become a national nightmare for many banks, business people, credit card companies, and their customers. "Plastic money is a real cancer which is growing daily in the United States. It is more difficult to cash a check at the bank for $100 than do a "sting" on credit card companies and make $250,000 in one week's work.

Although I was caught and convicted, it is not because the F. B. I. or the Dade County Public Safety Department [Credit Card Squad] did their work and caught me. I am here because a man that worked for me was arrested. Later, the attorney that I hired to represent him, black-mailed me for $50,000; finally, the attorney and the man worked out a deal with the government and sold me out.

Back in Cuba many years ago, someone very close to me told me that I was like the phoenix bird and that I will have different cycles in my life; and that someday I was going to be burned in the Temple of the Sun, like the phoenix did; that everyone thought I was dead, but out of the ashes I was born again, this time stronger. How right he was. I have decided to change my ways and repay justice and the society in which we live.

My only wish and desire is that in the near future, I will not be known as the best "sting artist" that everybody said I was, but as the best specialist in fighting credit card frauds and other related frauds that I can be; so my family and my children can once again be proud of me and not ashamed as they are now. I am sure you are well aware of my notorious past; and with no reservations whatsoever, I shall try to help and answer all your questions to the best of my ability, so help me God.

Mr. HUGHES. Would you tell us, first of all, how you got involved in this scheme, and what the scheme was, without naming companies or victims?

Mr. HOYO. I don't recall the number of victims. The first scheme that I did, I made a quarter of a million dollars. The name of the company was Check Guard Corp. This particular scheme—we run just one ad at the Wall Street Journal, and within two weeks I made a quarter of a million dollars. Six months after that, I did the same scheme but a little bit different. This particular scheme that I did first, I did what is called through a mail order. I did not use this particular machine that you see next to me. I didn't use any credit card. I just used the numbers and the names of the people that called me to purchase the particular items that I was selling at the Wall Street Journal. I just fill it out by pen and send it to American Express—where it said signature, I just put mail order, and they went ahead and paid me a quarter of a million dollars.

Mr. HUGHES. What did the ad in the Journal say?

Mr. HOYO. That particular ad I was selling a color TV, AM/FM stereo tape for $199. That particular TV cost me $220. I bought only fifty of them, and I sent it to the people that were screaming more at me

Mr. HUGHES. And what did you do when people responded to the ad——

Mr. HOYO. I went ahead and printed a card that says that I was going to be a little bit late in my delivery; instead of it taking me 6 weeks, it will take me 10 weeks. If you didn't want that I will go ahead and reimburse with their American Express; and that is exactly what I did. I sent everybody—I reimbursed through American Express telling them I was very sorry I could not. But at that time, I already charged those people probably 10 times the amount of money.

Mr. HUGHES. What advice do you have to people that write in to ads like that to make sure that they don't get bilked out of $199?

Mr. HOYO. I think you have to be extremely careful who you buy from in the mail order, extremely careful—you have to check this company out. I want you to know that—probably Mr. Ortega here knows that in the second company that I opened up, I even had a D&B report, which was Dun & Bradstreet report, this company being opened 7 years. And we were probably worth $8 million, and we have offices all over Florida. And if you check me out, this company will be a very good and legitimate company, if you check me out by paper, though.

Mr. HUGHES. You mentioned in your prepared statement that you were approached by members of organized crime that were interested in your expertise. Can you share with us just how deeply involved organized crime is in this whole area of credit card fraud?

Mr. HOYO. I think that in south Florida the problem with drugs are getting to be very bad, so people are changing the way, and criminals are going more into an easier type of market. And credit cards are a very easy market. It is very easy to make a lot of money with plastic money. And people are going to that market instead of going to other markets and there are people that with organized crime that have been approached by them to go ahead and do.

As a matter of fact, after I was going to finish my American Express job, I was going to go ahead and hit Southeast Bank for about $4 million. I would like to tell you something else—I already met with the people from the Southeast Bank. I told them exactly what I was going to do this past Monday and they went ahead and told me not to say anything because that still could be done, and they would lose the $4 million. I am trying to help them right now in stopping their credit card fraud at the bank.

Mr. HUGHES. You indicated that you were asking a $100,000 retainer for your services.

Mr. HOYO. That was in other frauds that I was involved in, sir, and not in this particular.

Mr. HUGHES. Not in this particular area?

Mr. HOYO. No, nobody wants to pay me $100,000.

Mr. HUGHES. That is what I understood, that you were basically a consultant as well as your own entrepreneur.

Mr. HOYO. Well, somebody would have given me the $100,000, I would have gone ahead and taken it, but it was more profitable to do it by myself than to get $100,000 from somebody else.

Mr. HUGHES. How long were you in the business?

Mr. HOYO. Frauds or credit card frauds, sir?

Mr. HUGHES. Credit card frauds.

Mr. HOYO. I was in about a year, less than a year.

Mr. HUGHES. Less than a year. And your most successful scam was in a period of 7 or 8 days?

Mr. HOYO. I was making a quarter of a million dollars every 8 days.

Mr. HUGHES. Every 8 days?

Mr. HOYO. Yes; I made a half a million dollars; from the second scam—I made on the first scam half a million dollars. And I was preparing my third scam for around $4 million or $5 million.

Mr. HUGHES. You had three scams altogether?

Mr. HOYO. No, I was going to, but I was stopped.

Mr. HUGHES. The third was interrupted?

Mr. HOYO. Yes, sir; it was interrupted.

Mr. HUGHES. It is your position now that this was fortunate.

Mr. HOYO. Well, I am glad it happened, Congressman, believe it or not.

Mr. HUGHES. The gentleman from Michigan.

Mr. SAWYER. You apparently had quite a lot of preparatory education before getting into the credit card scam.

Mr. HOYO. I guess I was a professional con artist, sir; that's what you call what I was.

Mr. SAWYER. For how long?

Mr. HOYO. For 6 years.

Mr. SAWYER. And did you make a lot of money at these other ones, too, while you were building up to the credit card?

Mr. HOYO. I will let Mr. Ortega let you know about that. I guess I lived pretty well, sir.

Mr. SAWYER. In a newspaper article I read about one of your two credit card scams indicated that none of the moneys or properties had ever been recovered.

Mr. HOYO. The properties are the credit card. Those I threw in the ocean. The money has not been recovered, no.

Mr. SAWYER. Where is the money?

Mr. HOYO. I don't have any money, sir. I don't know where the money is. I spent it.

Mr. SAWYER. What did you do with it?

Mr. HOYO. I lived very wealthy in Miami. I lived in half a million-dollar homes; I have very expensive cars, and very expensive taste.

Mr. SAWYER. I presume all this money was tax-free, too, right?

Mr. HOYO. Yes, sir; I haven't been charged yet.

Mr. SAWYER. You didn't pay any income taxes on this, I assume?

Mr. HOYO. No, sir; I don't have any money to pay income taxes.

Well!!! Arturo Hoyo, aka The Plastic Magician, had another day in court, but this time not fighting for his freedom. No!!! This time it was documenting his legacy as one of the greatest con-artists of the 20th century. Although he wasn't being totally truthful when it came to his motives for his appearance in front of the judiciary committee. Yes!!! It was voluntary, but wanting to be known as the greatest credit card specialist in helping banks and credit card companies avoid credit card fraud and other scams, along with landing a job as a consultant for a major bank or credit card company upon his release was the furthest thing from the truth, but what Arturo believed the committee wanted to hear.

For as it turned out, The Plastic Magician is flying free once again and his first moves upon his release from Federal Prison after serving eight years were moves back to his old ways in preparing for his new sting, and character one, Mr. Bacardi!!! Starting with Mr. Bacardi and a million-dollar sting to start his new found freedom!!! I truly feel sorry for the banking and credit card companies, along with all the unsuspected customers who fall prey to his scams, but all you can say is you got ripped off by the Best!!!

This was a story that needed to be told. Thank you for your time and interest in this story about one of the greatest scam artists of the twentieth century. So happy he came into my life and that I shared a little of his.

The End

By Ronnie Berke

ABOUT THE AUTHOR

RONALD J. BERKOWITZ was born of the Jewish faith in Miami beach, Florida but was raised in the Bronx, New York since the age of five. He has been a drug dealer and smuggler most of his life, even though he maintained steady and prestigious jobs in the hospitality and financial fields. He started working on Wall Street as a specialist clerk on the floor of the N.Y.S.E. at post 13, where he handled books for AT&T, McDonald Douglas and Sprague Electric. He was still selling marijuana on the streets of New York City and to stock brokers before the opening bell. After work, he would be attending Hunter College and New York School of Finance before getting drafted in 1967.

He served 18 months in Vietnam with the US Army, twelve of which were spent in an infantry company called the "Swamp Rats". It was there where after a firefight that lasted three days, against a North Vietnamese division in May of 1968 that left him with 40% disabilities. He was then transferred and given another assignment as an SG with an MP company in Saigon riding around the city in an MP Jeep with an M60 machine gun mounted on the front hood, protecting servicemen and civilians, and making sure they were out of the bars and off the street by the 10PM curfew.

He started sending marijuana back to friends in the states in already rolled cigarettes, 10 to a pack, 10 packs in a Martell Cognac box for $200.00. Then he would exchange the American money for Vietnamese money and get twice the amount on the black market. When he landed in Bakersfield, CA. on his birthday, April 23, 1969, he had $26,500 in his pocket. That was the start of his smuggler career in the United States.

In 1977, he moved down to Florida to take care of his dying parents leaving his job at the Playboy Club in Manhattan as a bartender. Once in Florida, he began smuggling marijuana and cocaine from Jamaica and Colombia on a larger scale, all the while maintaining a manager's position at Bobby Rubino's Place for Ribs in Ft. Lauderdale.

In 1980, after his second trial for cocaine, winning the first one in New York, but this time the Feds gave him 23 years for his role as a drug ring leader, trafficking on the east coast of the United States. The sentence came after being held without bond by Federal Judge Norman Roettger, who ruled he was a menace to the community. He started doing his time in F.C.I. Tallahassee in May of 1980. That is where he met and befriended Arturo Hoyo in the summer of 1983, when Arthur came there having been sentenced to 8 years for credit card fraud.

This is the story of his life up to his incarceration as one of the greatest impersonators and scam artists of the 20th century. As for the author, Ronald J. Berkowitz, served a total of 10 ½ years in federal prison. He has managed to stay out of jail and live a productive life without fear of going back to prison for illegal activity. This is a story he feels needs to be told as Arturo Hoyo was the most interesting and memorable person he has ever met.

Still looking good in 2018.

The Martel Cognac $200.00 Box.

Enemy flag captured after three days of fighting.

Lit up in Vietnam.

CPSIA information can be obtained
at www.ICGtesting.com
Printed in the USA
LVHW072142231121
704307LV00032B/591